Pregnancy Prayers

Pregnancy Prayers: Praying through Pregnancy and Beyond

2015 © Mandy Rose-Chambers

All rights reserved. No part of this book may be reproduced without express written consent of the author.

ISBN 978-0-9954959-0-6 Paperback

ISBN 978-0-9954959-1-3 Kindle

Scripture quotations from The Authorized (King James) Version. Rights in the Authorized Version in the United Kingdom are vested in the Crown. Reproduced by permission of the Crown's patentee, Cambridge University Press.

Publishing and Design Services | MelindaMartin.me

Pregnancy Prayers

Praying through Pregnancy & Beyond

Mandy Rose-Chambers

Dedication

For all my children and the blessings still to come.

Contents

Foreword 1

Section One: Why Pray 3

Section Two: Praying for a Baby 9

Section Three: Development 19

Section Four: Protection 29

Section Five: Peace 39

Section Six: Patience 47

Section Seven: Healing 53

Section Eight: Birth 67

Section Nine: Blessings 75

Section Ten: Salvation 87

Section Eleven: Week-By-Week 95

Section Twelve: Our Story 121

References 143

Foreword

Pregnancy is a wonderful time, even with the ups and downs of morning sickness, weight gain, tiredness and worries; it is also a wonderful time to be in awe of the miracle of a baby being formed. At the back of the book, there is a week-by-week guide to the changes and growth occurring within the foetus as your pregnancy progresses. I remember having to go for a scan at 5 weeks with our daughter, and even at 5 weeks we could visibly see the heart beating and see the small group of her being forming within the womb.

When we see the detail that God has placed in how we are formed, we can't help but to be in wonder at His great care for us. In Psalm 8, David declares, "What is man that you are mindful of him, the son of man that you think about us?"

I hope that these verses will encourage you in the 40-week journey through your pregnancy. Not every scripture verse will seem relevant to you, but it is about finding those that grip your spirit that you can take hold of and hide in your heart because it's what you believe God has said to you personally. I have written a chapter called *Our Story*, a time when we had to find and then apply God's word in a situation with one of our children. We called out to God. He heard us and attended to our cry, and it is what we are always grateful for beyond word or measure.

My God bless you on your journey.

Pregnancy Prayers

Section One: Why Pray

Jesus was born in Bethlehem, which means *house of bread*. Jesus himself is called the *bread of life* (John 6:48). If we would take His word and remind Him of His word, He promises that His word will never return to Him void (Isaiah 55:11). His word sustains us and gives life as we pray over our children. He alone is the hope for their future and salvation (Jonah 2:9).

Use God's word when praying because it is a powerful weapon against the enemy. It strengthens our hearts when we pray to our Lord and saviour because it reminds us of His great promises and God is not a man that he would lie (Numbers 23:19).

I waited patiently for the Lord; and He inclined unto me, and heard my cry.

Psalm 40:1

Except the Lord build the house, they labour in vain that build it: except the Lord keep the city, the watchman waketh but in vain.

Psalm 127:1

How precious also are thy thoughts unto me, O God! How great is the sum of them!

Psalm 139:17

The Lord is righteous in all his ways, and holy in all his works. The Lord is nigh unto all them that call upon him, to all that call upon him in truth.

Psalm 145: 17,18

Surely He scorneth the scorners: but He giveth grace unto the lowly.

Proverbs 3:34

For the word of God is quick, and powerful, and sharper than any two-edged sword.

Hebrews 4:12

Word to Encourage

*I lift up mine eyes unto the hills,
from whence cometh my help?
My help cometh from the Lord,
which made Heaven and Earth.
He will not suffer thy foot to be moved:
He that keepeth Israel shall either slumber nor
sleep. The Lord is thy keeper:
the Lord is thy shade upon thy right hand.
The sun shall not smite thee by day,
nor the moon by night.
The Lord shall preserve thee from all evil:
He shall preserve thy soul.
The Lord shall preserve thy going out and thy
coming in from this time forth,
and even for evermore.*

Psalm 121

Prayer Starter:

Thank you, Lord, that You give me the humility to come before You and lay my requests at Your feet. I acknowledge that my help comes from the Lord, the maker of Heaven and Earth (Psalm 121). You alone can keep my foot from slipping. You alone know the cry of my heart, even before the words have reached my lips (Psalm 139:4).

Help me to come before You with a clean heart and pure motives. Lord, I ask for …

Pregnancy Prayers

Prayer notes:

Pregnancy Prayers

Section Two:

Praying for a Baby

"Shall I bring to birth, and not cause to bring forth? " saith the Lord. "Shall I cause to bring forth, and shut the womb?" saith thy God.

Isaiah 66:9

We know that we can trust that God will not withhold any good thing from us when we ask (Psalm 84:11). Children are a good thing! They are a heritage from the Lord (Psalm 127:3) and we can trust in His word and not give up. We can be assured that God will grant us the desires of our hearts if we commit our ways to Him (Psalm 37:4; Proverbs 16:3).

It is disappointing to wait months or even years for a child, but we can also trust that God's timing is perfect. In Psalm 116:2, David says, "He inclined His ear to me," and you can be sure that God hears your prayers, too.

And God blessed them,
and God said unto them,
Be fruitful, and multiply,
and replenish the earth, and subdue it:

Genesis 1:28

And God blessed Noah and his sons, and said
unto them, "Be fruitful, and multiply,
and replenish the earth."

Genesis 9:1

And Isaac intreated
(beg, implore, asked for earnestly)
the Lord for his wife, because she was barren:
and the Lord was intreated of him,
and Rebekah his wife conceived.

Genesis 25:21

And He lifted up his eyes, and saw the women
and the children; and said,
"Who are those with thee?" And He said,
"The children which God hath
graciously given thy servant."

Genesis 33:5

*Ye shall serve the Lord your God, and He shall
bless thy bread, and thy water;
and I will take sickness away from
the midst of thee.*

         Exodus 23:25

*Thou shalt be blessed above all people: there
shall not be male or female barren among you,
or among your cattle.*

         Deuteronomy 7:14

*And it shall come to pass, if thou shalt hearken
diligently unto the voice of the Lord thy God, to
observe and to do all his commandments which
I command thee this day, that the Lord thy
God will set thee on high above
all nations of the earth:
And all these blessings shall come on thee,
and overtake thee, if thou shalt hearken unto the
voice of the Lord thy God.
Blessed shalt thou be in the city,
and blessed shalt thou be in the field.
Blessed shall be the fruit of thy body
(your womb)
And the Lord shall make thee plenteous in
goods, in the fruit of thy body*

         Deuteronomy 28:1-4, 11

So Boaz took Ruth, and she was his wife: and when He went in unto her, the Lord gave her conception, and she bare a son.

          Ruth 4:13

And she said, Let thine handmaid find grace in thy sight. So the woman went her way, and did eat, and her countenance was no more sad…… Wherefore it came to pass, when the time was come about after Hannah had conceived, that she bare a son, and called his name Samuel, saying, Because I have asked him of the Lord.

         1 Samuel 1:18,20

Thou shalt know also that thy seed shall be great, and thine offspring as the grass of the earth.

         Job 5:25

Delight thyself also in the Lord: and He shall give thee the desires of thine heart.

         Psalm 37:4

For the Lord God is a sun and shield: the Lord will give grace and glory: no good thing will He withhold from them that walk uprightly.

         Psalm 84:11

The Lord shall give that which is good; and our land shall yield her increase.

> Psalm 85:12

And He increased his people greatly; and made them stronger than their enemies.

> Psalm 105:24

He maketh the barren woman to keep house, and to be a joyful mother of children.

> Psalm 113:9

*Lo, children are an heritage of the Lord: and the fruit of the womb is his reward. As arrows are in the hand of a mighty man;
so are children of the youth.*

> Psalm 127:3,4

Thy wife shall be as a fruitful vine by the sides of thine house: thy children like olive plants round about thy table.

> Psalm 128:3

I love them that love me; and those that seek me early shall find me

> Proverbs 8:17

For thus saith the Lord that created the heavens;
God himself that formed the earth and made it;
He hath established it, He created it not in vain,
He formed it to be inhabited: I am the Lord;
and there is none else.

Isaiah 45:18

Sing, O barren, thou that didst not bear;
break forth into singing, and cry aloud,
thou that didst not travail with child:
for more are the children of the desolate than
the children of the married wife, saith the Lord.
Enlarge the place of thy tent, and let them
stretch forth the curtains of thine habitations:
spare not, lengthen thy cords,
and strengthen thy stakes;
For thou shalt break forth on the right hand
and on the left; and thy seed shall inherit the
Gentiles, and make the desolate cities
to be inhabited.

Isaiah 54: 1-3

But the angel said unto him, Fear not,
Zacharias: for thy prayer is heard

Luke 1:13

Now faith is the substance of things hoped for, the evidence of things not seen.

Hebrews 11:1

So then neither is He that planteth any thing, neither He that watereth; but God that giveth the increase.

1 Corinthians 3:7

Prayer Starter:

Thank You, Lord, that You said that if we call out to You with a pure heart You will hear my prayer. I come before You now; please hear my cry. I thank You that You are a God who cares about everything that happens in my life. You are my great shepherd. Please lead me as I pray.

Firstly, I renounce any negative word I have spoken over myself or any negative word spoken over me by someone else. I ask that if there have been areas where I have sinned, complaining about any provision You have given me, then I ask for forgiveness now.

I thank You that I can come and make my request known for a baby. in your word, Lord, You said that You are our good father and know how to give good things to his children (Matthew 7:9). You heard the cry of Rebekah and Hannah and You blessed them with children, I know You are not a respecter of persons; please, Lord, consider my request.

I acknowledge that it is You who opens and closes wombs, and I pray that by your grace my womb is open to conceive. Help give me patience, knowing that your timing is perfect. Please help me to be patient, and I acknowledge that children are a blessing to You.

I pray this in Jesus' precious name.

Personal Notes:

Section Three: Development

*Now the God of hope fill you
with all joy and peace in believing, that ye may
abound in hope,
through the power of the Holy Ghost.*

Romans 15:13

Pregnancy Prayers

Prayer Scriptures for Development

God made us. He called us even before we were born. In the following verses, God says that He not only formed us but He knows us each individually and intricately. Job acknowledges that he has the breath of God within him (Job 27:3) and that it was God who formed him in the womb (Job 31:15). We can trust God and His word to give us the scriptures to pray over our children, even while they are growing and developing in the womb.

In Isaiah 45:19 it says, " I am the lord, and there is no other. I have not spoken in secret from somewhere in a land of darkness; I have not said to Jacob's descendants, 'seek me in vain.' I, the lord, speak the truth: I declare what is right." God's word is truth, active and powerful to declare that which we hope into an area we cannot see.

And the Lord God formed man of the dust of the ground, and breathed into his nostrils the breath of life; and man became a living soul.

Genesis 2:7

And the Lord said unto him, Who hath made man's mouth? or who maketh the dumb, or deaf, or the seeing, or the blind? have not I the Lord?

Exodus 4:11

In whose hand is the soul of every living thing, and the breath of all mankind.

Job 12:10

The spirit of God hath made me, and the breath of the Almighty hath given me life.

Job 33:4

Thy mercy, O Lord, is in the heavens; and thy faithfulness reacheth unto the clouds. Thy righteousness is like the great mountains; thy judgments are a great deep: O Lord, thou preservest man and beast. How excellent is thy lovingkindness, O God! therefore the children of men put their trust under the shadow of thy wings.

Psalm 36:5-7

Know ye that the Lord He is God: it is He that hath made us, and not we ourselves; we are his people, and the sheep of his pasture.

Psalm 100:3

For thou hast possessed my reins: thou hast covered me in my mother's womb. I will praise thee; for I am fearfully and wonderfully made: marvellous are thy works; and that my soul knoweth right well. My substance was not hid from thee, when I was made in secret, and curiously wrought in the lowest parts of the earth. Thine eyes did see my substance, yet being unperfect; and in thy book all my members were written, which in continuance were fashioned, when as yet there was none of them.

Psalm 139:13-16

The hearing ear, and the seeing eye, the Lord hath made even both of them.

Proverbs 20:12

As thou knowest not what is the way of the spirit, nor how the bones do grow in the womb of her that is with child: even so thou knowest not the works of God who maketh all.

Ecclesiastes 11:5

Thus saith God the Lord, He that created the heavens, and stretched them out; He that spread forth the earth, and that which cometh out of it; He that giveth breath unto the people upon it, and spirit to them that walk therein:

Isaiah 42:5

But now thus saith the Lord that created thee, O Jacob, and He that formed thee, O Israel, Fear not: for I have redeemed thee, I have called thee by thy name; thou art mine.

Isaiah 43:1

Even every one that is called by my name: for I have created him for my glory, I have formed him; yea, I have made him.

Isaiah 43:7

No weapon that is formed against thee shall prosper; and every tongue that shall rise against thee in judgment thou shalt condemn.

Isaiah 54:17

And the Lord shall guide thee continually, and satisfy thy soul in drought, and make fat thy bones: and thou shalt be like a watered garden, and like a spring of water, whose waters fail not.

Isaiah 58:11

But now, O Lord, thou art our father; we are the clay, and thou our potter; and we all are the work of thy hand.

Isaiah 64:8

Before I formed thee in the belly I knew thee;

Jeremiah 1:5

O come, let us worship and bow down: let us kneel before the Lord our maker. For He is our God; and we are the people of his pasture, and the sheep of his hand.

Psalm 95:6,7

Prayer Starter:

Thank You, Lord, that You are my shepherd. I am a sheep under your great and almighty care. I ask, Lord, too, that You would watch over the baby You have given me as it develops day by day. Thank You for the wonderful miracle that is happening inside my body right now. Help me to take care of myself with proper eating habits and bodily care. Thank You, Lord, that I can cast my cares upon You (Psalm 55:22) so that I can have peace these nine months knowing that my baby, family, and myself are in your care.

Thank You, Lord, that You watch over every developmental detail of this precious baby and this week I specifically pray for ...

(Perhaps looking at the developmental week-by-week section, you can pray specifically each week)

Personal Notes:

Pregnancy Prayers

Section Four: Protection

He that dwelleth in the secret place of the most High, shall abide under the shadow of the Almighty

Psalm 91:1

Pregnancy Prayers

Scripture Verses for Protection

I am with thee, and will keep thee in all places whither thou goest

                                        Genesis 28:15

Be strong and of a good courage, fear not, nor be afraid of them: for the Lord thy God,
He it is that doth go with thee; He will not fail thee, nor forsake thee.

                               Deuteronomy 31:6

Mine eyes are ever toward the Lord; for He shall pluck my feet out of the net.

                                          Psalm 25:15

The Lord is my light and my salvation; whom shall I fear? The Lord is the strength of my life; of whom shall I be afraid?

                                            Psalm 27:1

The Lord is my shepherd; I shall not want. He maketh me to lie down in green pastures: He leadeth me beside the still waters.
He restoreth my soul: He leadeth me in the paths of righteousness for his name's sake.

Yea, though I walk through the valley of the shadow of death, I will fear no evil: for thou art with me; thy rod and thy staff they comfort me.

Psalm 23:1-4

For in the time of trouble He shall hide me in his pavilion: in the secret of his tabernacle shall He hide me; He shall set me up upon a rock.

Psalm 27:5

The Lord is my strength and my shield; my heart trusted in him, and I am helped

Psalm 28:7

The angel of the Lord encampeth round about them that fear him, and delivereth them.

Psalm 34:7

Behold, God is mine helper: the Lord is with them that uphold my soul.

Psalm 54:4

Thou hast beset (covered) me behind and before, and laid thine hand upon me.

Psalm 139:5

Fear thou not; for I am with thee: be not dismayed; for I am thy God: I will strengthen thee; yea, I will help thee; yea, I will uphold thee with the right hand of my righteousness.

Isaiah 41:10

Word to Encourage

He that dwelleth in the secret place of the most High shall abide under the shadow of the Almighty. I will say of the Lord, He is my refuge and my fortress: my God; in him will I trust. Surely He shall deliver thee from the snare of the fowler, and from the noisome pestilence. He shall cover thee with his feathers, and under his wings shalt thou trust: his truth shall be thy shield and buckler.

Thou shalt not be afraid for the terror by night; nor for the arrow that flieth by day; Nor for the pestilence that walketh in darkness; nor for the destruction that wasteth at noonday. A thousand shall fall at thy side, and ten thousand at thy right hand; but it shall not come nigh thee.

Only with thine eyes shalt thou behold and see the reward of the wicked. Because thou hast made the Lord, which is my refuge, even the most High, thy habitation; There shall no evil befall thee, neither shall any plague come nigh thy dwelling.

For He shall give his angels charge over thee, to keep thee in all thy ways. They shall bear thee up in their hands, lest thou dash thy foot against a stone. Thou shalt tread upon the lion and adder: the young lion and the dragon shalt thou trample under feet.

Because He hath set his love upon me, therefore will I deliver him: I will set him on high, because He hath known my name. He shall call upon me, and I will answer him: I will be with him in trouble; I will deliver him, and honour him. With long life will I satisfy him, and shew him my salvation.

Psalm 91

Prayer Starters:

Lord, help me to dwell in Your secret place of prayer and praise. I thank You that You see my baby in the secret place within my womb and ask that You would watch over him/her as he develops. Thank You, Lord, that daily You would keep me from all harm. Lord, hem me in behind and in front (Psalm 139:5). Thank You, Lord, that as this little one develops that he/she would know Your voice.

Lord, rejoice over my baby (and family) with singing and may my baby rest in Your love as You joy over him/her with singing (Zephaniah 3:17).

Thank You that Your love and care would not just be for now but throughout his/her life.

Pregnancy Prayers

Personal Notes:

Pregnancy Prayers

Section Five: Peace

Blessed be the Lord, who hath given rest unto His people Israel, according to all that He promised. There hath not failed one word of all his good promise, which He promised by the hand of Moses his servant.

1 Kings 8: 56

Pregnancy Prayers

The Peace of God Which Passes Understanding

The eternal God is thy refuge, and underneath are the everlasting arms: and He shall thrust out the enemy from before thee; and shall say, "Destroy them."

Deuteronomy 33:27

God is my strength and power: and He maketh my way perfect.

2 Samuel 22:33

God is our refuge and strength, a very present help in trouble. Therefore will not we fear, though the earth be removed, and though the mountains be carried into the midst of the sea

Psalm 46:1-2

The Lord of hosts is with us; the God of Jacob is our refuge.

Psalm 46:7

Cast thy burden upon the Lord, and He shall sustain thee: He shall never suffer the righteous to be moved.

         Psalm 55:22

O Lord God of hosts, who is a strong Lord like unto thee? or to thy faithfulness round about thee?

         Psalm 89:8

Like as a father pitieth his children, so the Lord pitieth them that fear him. For He knoweth our frame; He remembereth that we are dust. But the mercy of the Lord is from everlasting to everlasting upon them that fear him, and his righteousness unto children's children

         Psalm 103:13,14,17

Great peace have they which love thy law: and nothing shall offend them.

         Psalm 119:165

Thou wilt keep him in perfect peace, whose mind is stayed on thee: because He trusteth in thee. Trust ye in the Lord for ever: for in the Lord Jehovah is everlasting strength

         Isaiah 26:3,4

Fear thou not; for I am with thee: be not dismayed; for I am thy God: I will strengthen thee; yea, I will help thee; yea, I will uphold thee with the right hand of my righteousness.

Isaiah 41:10

Fear not: for I have redeemed thee, I have called thee by thy name; thou art mine. When thou passest through the waters, I will be with thee; and through the rivers, they shall not overflow thee: when thou walkest through the fire, thou shalt not be burned; neither shall the flame kindle upon thee. For I am the Lord thy God, the Holy One of Israel, thy Saviour

Isaiah 43:1-3

Thus saith the Lord that made thee, and formed thee from the womb, which will help thee; Fear not

Isaiah 44:2

Can a woman forget her sucking child, that she should not have compassion on the son of her womb? yea, they may forget, yet will I not forget thee. Behold, I have graven thee upon the palms of my hands; thy walls are continually before me.

Isaiah 49:15,16

I, even I, am He that comforteth you

                                              Isaiah 51:12

And all thy children shall be taught of the Lord; and great shall be the peace of thy children.

                                              Isaiah 54:13

Peace, peace to him that is far off, and to him that is near, saith the Lord

                                              Isaiah 57:19b

Prayer Starter:

Thank You, Lord, that You said that You would keep those in perfect peace whose mind is fixed on You (Isaiah 26:3). Help me to keep my mind fixed on You and the promises in Your word as I give over to You the worries in my mind and those thoughts that lay heavy on my heart. Help me to take Your burden for it is light (Matthew 11:29-30). Help me to trust that I am ever in Your care and that You have an answer to my every need.

Lord, I present these things before You and ask for Your help....

Personal Notes:

Section Six: Patience

*Wait on the Lord: be of good courage,
and He shall strengthen thine heart:
wait, I say, on the Lord.*

Psalm 27:14

Pregnancy Prayers

Scriptures for Patience, Especially in the Last Few Weeks

Rejoicing in hope; patient in tribulation; continuing in prayer;

Romans 12:12

My grace is sufficient for thee: for my strength is made perfect in weakness. Most gladly therefore will I rather glory in my infirmities, that the power of Christ may rest upon me.

2 Corinthians 12:9

But the fruit of the Spirit is love, joy, peace, longsuffering, gentleness, goodness, faith.

Galatians 5:22

Charity (love)…..Beareth all things, believeth all things, hopeth all things, endureth all things. Love never fails.

1 Corinthians 13:7

Let us not be weary in well doing: for in due season we shall reap, if we faint not.

Galatians 6:9

Be careful for nothing; but in every thing by prayer and supplication with thanksgiving let your requests be made known unto God. And the peace of God, which passeth all understanding, shall keep your hearts and minds through Christ Jesus.

Philippians 4:6-7

I can do all things through Christ which strengtheneth me.

Philippians 4:13

Strengthened with all might, according to his glorious power, unto all patience and longsuffering with joyfulness

Colossians 1:11

But they that wait upon the Lord shall renew their strength; they shall mount up with wings as eagles; they shall run, and not be weary; and they shall walk, and not faint.

Isaiah 40:31

Prayer Starter:

Thank You, Lord, that You said that You will never leave us nor forsake us (Hebrews 13:5). I pray that You, as my Prince of Peace will become more real to me at this time when I need Your peace in my heart and mind. Lord, help me to realize that all things are in Your hand and that You do Your holy will. Lord, help me not to grow weary as I worry about matters too hard for me to understand or guess the result. Help me not worry about the days ahead, the birth, and development but let me know that peace in really trusting in You and resting in Your care. Let me trust in Your promise that You go before me, that You will not forsake or fail me (Deuteronomy 31:6).

Lord, I bring to You the worries I am facing now, these include:

Personal Notes:

Section Seven: Healing

Pregnancy Prayers

Healing for Foetus, Post Partum, Baby

As strenuous as a normal pregnancy can be, news that a pregnancy is not developing as expected can be devastating. To discover that your precious baby might need medical attention during or after the birth can cause much pain and upset.

In that moment of truth, it can feel like your whole world is shattered. It is at this time that we need to let God speak into our hearts, "peace, be still" (Mark 4:39).

There are many stories; I am sure each person has their own story of grief and pain. I think it is humbling and amazing how God comes through, each time in a different way. It is when His word grips your heart and you know that He won't let you go that you continue on the road, knowing that even when you feel like you are crawling along, He is there. He is holding you in the palm of His hand.

But unto you that fear my name shall the Sun of righteousness arise with healing in his wings

Malachi 4:2

Ye shall serve the Lord your God, and He shall bless thy bread, and thy water; and I will take sickness away from the midst of thee. There shall nothing cast (miscarry) their young, nor be barren, in thy land: the number of thy days I will fulfil. (I will give you a full lifespan)

Exodus 23:25,26

For the Lord thy God hath blessed thee in all the works of thy hand: He knoweth thy walking through this great wilderness: these forty years the Lord thy God hath been with thee; thou hast lacked nothing.

Deuteronomy 2:7

But ye that did cleave (held fast) unto the Lord your God are alive every one of you this day.

Deuteronomy 4:4

For the Lord thy God is a merciful God; He will not forsake thee, neither destroy thee, nor forget the covenant of thy fathers which He sware unto them.

Deuteronomy 4:31

Thou shalt keep therefore his statutes, and his commandments, which I command thee this day, that it may go well with thee, and with thy children after thee, and that thou mayest prolong thy days upon the earth, which the Lord thy God giveth thee, for ever.

                              Deuteronomy 4:40

Ye shall walk in all the ways which the Lord your God hath commanded you, that ye may live, and that it may be well with you, and that ye may prolong your days in the land which ye shall possess.

                              Deuteronomy 5:33

Depart from me, all ye workers of iniquity;(you who do evil) for the Lord hath heard the voice of my weeping. The Lord hath heard my supplication; (to ask or beg) the Lord will receive my prayer. Let all mine enemies be ashamed and sore vexed: (annoyed, frustrated) let them return and be ashamed suddenly.

                              Psalm 6:8-10

It is God that girdeth (arms) me with strength, and maketh my way perfect. He maketh my feet like hinds'(deer) feet, and setteth me upon my high places.He teacheth my hands to war, so that a bow of steel is broken by mine arms. Thou

*hast also given me the shield of thy salvation:
and thy right hand hath holden me up, and
thy gentleness hath made me great. Thou hast
enlarged my steps under me,
that my feet did not slip.*

Psalm 18:32-36

*Though I walk through the valley of the shadow
of death, I will fear no evil: for thou art with
me; thy rod and thy staff they comfort me. Thou
preparest a table before me in the presence of
mine enemies: thou anointest my head with oil;
my cup runneth over. Surely goodness and mercy
shall follow me all the days of my life: and I will
dwell in the house of the Lord for ever.*

Psalm 23:4-6

*The Lord is their strength, and He is the saving
strength of his anointed.*

Psalm 28:8

*I sought the Lord, and He heard me, and
delivered me from all my fears.
They looked unto Him, and were lightened: and
their faces were not ashamed.
This poor man cried, and the Lord heard him,
and saved him out of all his troubles.
The angel of the Lord encampeth round about
them that fear Him, and delivereth them.*

*O taste and see that the Lord is good:
blessed is the man that trusteth in Him.
O fear the Lord, ye his saints:
for there is no want to them that fear him.
The young lions do lack, and suffer hunger: but
they that seek the Lord shall
not want any good thing.*

                                            Psalm 34:4-10

*Thy righteousness is like the great mountains;
thy judgments are a great deep: O Lord, thou
preservest man and beast. How excellent is thy
lovingkindness, O God! therefore
the children of men put their trust under the
shadow of thy wings.*

                                            Psalm 36:6-7

*But the salvation of the righteous is of the Lord:
He is their strength in the time of trouble. And
the Lord shall help them, and deliver them: He
shall deliver them from the wicked, and save
them, because they trust in him.*

                                            Psalm 37:39,40a

*Which holdeth (preserved) our soul in life, and
suffereth not our feet to be moved*

                                            Psalm 66:9

Blessed be the Lord, who daily loadeth us with benefits, even the God of our salvation. He that is our God is the God of salvation; and unto God the Lord belong the issues from death (escape from death).

Psalm 68:19-20

My flesh and my heart faileth: but God is the strength of my heart (life), and my portion for ever.

Psalm 73:26

Bless the Lord, O my soul, and forget not all his benefits: Who forgiveth all thine iniquities (sins); who healeth all thy diseases; Who redeemeth thy life from destruction; who crowneth thee with lovingkindness and tender mercies; Who satisfieth thy mouth with good things; so that thy youth is renewed like the eagle's.

Psalm 103:2-5

For thou hast been a strength to the poor, a strength to the needy in his distress, a refuge from the storm, a shadow from the heat.

Isaiah 25:4

He giveth power to the faint; and to them that have no might (weak) He increaseth strength.

Even the youths shall faint and be weary (tired), and the young men shall utterly fall: But they that wait upon the Lord shall renew their strength; they shall mount up with wings as eagles; they shall run, and not be weary; and they shall walk, and not faint.

Isaiah 40:29-31

Fear thou not; for I am with thee: be not dismayed; for I am thy God: I will strengthen thee; yea, I will help thee; yea, I will uphold thee with the right hand of my righteousness. For I the Lord thy God will hold thy right hand, saying unto thee, Fear not; I will help thee.

Isaiah 41:10,13

Surely He hath borne (carried) our griefs, and carried our sorrows: yet we did esteem him stricken, smitten of God, and afflicted. But He was wounded for our transgressions, He was bruised for our iniquities: the chastisement of our peace was upon him; and with his stripes we are healed. All we like sheep have gone astray; we have turned every one to his own way; and the Lord hath laid on him the iniquity of us all.

Isaiah 53:4-6

No weapon that is formed against thee shall prosper; and every tongue that shall rise against thee in judgment thou shalt condemn. This is the heritage of the servants of the Lord, and their righteousness (vindication) is of me, saith the Lord.

Isaiah 54:17

So shall my word be that goeth forth out of my mouth: it shall not return unto me void, but it shall accomplish that which I please, and it shall prosper (achieve, purpose)in the thing whereto I sent it.

Isaiah 55:11

Behold, I am the Lord, the God of all flesh: is there any thing too hard for me?

Jeremiah 32:27

How God anointed Jesus of Nazareth with the Holy Ghost and with power: who went about doing good, and healing all that were oppressed of the devil; for God was with him.

Acts 10:38

What shall we then say to these things? If God be for us, who can be against us? He that spared not his own Son, but delivered him up for us all, how shall He not with him also freely give us all things?

                                             Romans 8:31,32

For though we walk in the flesh, we do not war after the flesh: For the weapons of our warfare are not carnal, but mighty through God to the pulling down of strong holds; Casting down imaginations, and every high thing that exalteth itself against the knowledge of God, and bringing into captivity every thought to the obedience of Christ;

                                        2 Corinthians 10:3-4

Now unto him that is able to do exceeding abundantly above all that we ask or think, according to the power that worketh in us

                                                 Ephesians 3:20

Ye are of God, little children, and have overcome them: because greater is He that is in you, than He that is in the world.

                                                       1 John 4:4

For this purpose the Son of God was manifested, that He might destroy the works of the devil.

                                                   1 John 3:8b

Words to Encourage

Then shall thy light break forth as the morning, and thine health shall spring forth speedily: and thy righteousness shall go before thee; the glory of the Lord shall be thy reward.

Then shalt thou call, and the Lord shall answer; thou shalt cry, and He shall say, Here I am. If thou take away from the midst of thee the yoke, the putting forth of the finger, and speaking vanity;

And if thou draw out thy soul to the hungry, and satisfy the afflicted soul; then shall thy light rise in obscurity, and thy darkness be as the noon day:

And the Lord shall guide thee continually, and satisfy thy soul in drought, and make fat thy bones: and thou shalt be like a watered garden, and like a spring of water, whose waters fail not.

Isaiah 58:8-11

Prayer Starter:

Lord, at this moment I feel like I am being tossed about on the storms in my life. I don't know what to do, and I am probably not able to pray the most elegant prayer at this very moment. But I need Your help. Lord, You said that it was by Your stripes that we are healed. Lord, I trust Your word that this is so. Lord, guide me now and hold my heart close as I grapple with these feelings of fear and doubt.

In Joshua, You said, "Be strong and courageous. Do not be frightened, and do not be dismayed for You are with me wherever I go" (Joshua 1:9). Lord help me not to rely on my own strength at this time; help me to turn to You. In a time of trouble, You sent Hur and Aaron to hold up Moses' hands. Lord, please send people across my path to encourage, strengthen and support me in this battle that I/we face. Lord, I know that all Your ways are loving and faithful (Psalm 25:10) so help me trust You and know that You are a God of miracles and You can do all things – NOTHING is impossible for You (Matthew 19:26; Luke 1:37).

Personal Notes:

Section Eight: Birth

Pregnancy Prayers

Before Meeting Your Little One

But his bow abode in strength (his bow remained steady), and the arms of his hands were made strong by the hands of the mighty God of Jacob; (from thence is the shepherd, the stone of Israel:) Even by the God of thy father, who shall help thee; and by the Almighty, who shall bless thee with blessings of heaven above, blessings of the deep that lieth under, blessings of the breasts, and of the womb.

Genesis 49:24,25a

The Lord is my strength and song, and He is become my salvation

Exodus 15:2

Have not I commanded thee? Be strong and of a good courage; be not afraid, neither be thou dismayed: for the Lord thy God is with thee whithersoever thou goest.

Joshua 1:9

God is my strength and power: and He maketh my way perfect. He maketh my feet like hinds'(deer) feet: and setteth me upon my high places. He teacheth my hands to war; so that a bow of steel is broken by mine arms. Thou hast also given me the shield of thy salvation (victory).

                          2 Samuel 22:33-36a

I have set the Lord always before me: because He is at my right hand, I shall not be moved. Therefore my heart is glad, and my glory rejoiceth: my flesh also shall rest in hope.

                                    Psalm 16:8,9

But thou art He that took me out of the womb: thou didst make me hope when I was upon my mother's breasts. I was cast upon thee from the womb: thou art my God from my mother's belly.

                                      Psalm 22:9,10

The Lord is their strength, and He is the saving strength of his anointed.

                                        Psalm 28:8

Be of good courage, and He shall strengthen your heart, all ye that hope in the Lord.

                                        Psalm 31:24

My soul followeth hard after thee (my soul clings to thee): thy right hand upholdeth me.

Psalm 63:8

The Lord is nigh (near) unto all them that call upon him, to all that call upon him in truth. He will fulfil the desire of them that fear him: He also will hear their cry, and will save them. The Lord preserveth watches, keeps) all them that love him:

Psalm 145:18-20

*Hast thou not known?
Hast thou not heard, that the everlasting God, the Lord, the Creator of the ends of the earth, fainteth not, neither is weary?
There is no searching of his understanding. He giveth power to the faint; and to them that have no might He increaseth strength.
Even the youths shall faint and be weary, and the young men shall utterly fall:
But they that wait upon the
Lord shall renew their strength*

Isaiah 40:28-31a

Prayer Starter:

Lord, I know that You care about all aspects of my life. At this time, I bring to You the birth. I thank You that all things will go smoothly with the delivery and that You will give me the strength to endure the birth process and the pain. Thank You that You will put a hedge of protection around me and the baby throughout the process. I thank You for being with me through this pregnancy and know that You will not leave me at the last hurdle.

Thank You that after that pain we can welcome the new blessing in our life that we have eagerly waited to meet for the last nine months. Thank You that You will give my other children peace as they wait for the arrival of their new brother or sister.

We ask for love and acceptance in all of our hearts and that our new arrival will be well aware of the love from You and his/her family. I bring to You the midwife/doctor who will be there, and I pray that You will have Your angels surrounding us all.

Personal Notes:

Pregnancy Prayers

Section Nine: Blessings

Arise, shine; for thy light has come, and the glory of the Lord is risen upon thee.

Isaiah 60:1

Pregnancy Prayers

Speaking Blessing and Life

Obedience to God and His laws – Only if thou carefully hearken unto the voice of the Lord thy God, to observe to do all these commandments which I command thee this day. For the Lord thy God blesseth thee, as He promised thee: and thou shalt lend unto many nations, but thou shalt not borrow; and thou shalt reign over many nations, but they shall not reign over thee.

Deuteronomy 15:5,6

Your son or daughter will grow in favour both with the Lord, and also with men.

1 Samuel 2:26

I have been young, and now am old; yet have I not seen the righteous forsaken, nor his seed begging bread.

Psalm 37:25

Blessed is the man that walketh not in the counsel of the ungodly, nor standeth in the way of sinners, nor sitteth in the seat of the scornful. But his delight is in the law of the Lord; and in his law doth He meditate day and night.

And He shall be like a tree planted by the rivers of water, that bringeth forth his fruit in his season; his leaf also shall not wither; and whatsoever He doeth shall prosper. The ungodly are not so: but are like the chaff which the wind driveth away. Therefore the ungodly shall not stand in the judgment, nor sinners in the congregation of the righteous. For the Lord knoweth the way of the righteous: but the way of the ungodly shall perish.

Psalm 1

And the blood shall be to you for a token upon the houses where ye are: and when I see the blood, I will pass over you, and the plague shall not be upon you to destroy you

Exodus 12:13

This book of the law shall not depart out of thy mouth; but thou shalt meditate therein day and night, that thou mayest observe to do according to all that is written therein: for then thou shalt make thy way prosperous, and then thou shalt have good success.

Joshua 1:8

*The secret of the Lord is with them that fear him;
and He will shew them his covenant.*

         Psalm 25:14

*My foot standeth in an even place: in the
congregations will I bless the Lord.*

         Psalm 26:12

*O taste and see that the Lord is good: blessed is
the man that trusteth in him.*

         Psalm 34:8

*The steps of a good man are ordered by the Lord:
and He delighteth in his way*

         Psalm 37:23

*He shall not be afraid of evil tidings: his heart
is fixed, trusting in the Lord. His heart is
established, He shall not be afraid, until He see
his desire upon his enemies.*

         Psalm 112:7-8

*Thy word is a lamp unto my feet,
and a light unto my path.*

         Psalm 119:105

*The Lord will perfect that which concerneth me
(the lord will fulfil His purpose for me): thy
mercy, O Lord, endureth for ever: forsake not the
works of thine own hands.*

Psalm 138:8

*Call unto me, and I will answer thee, and show
thee great and mighty things,
which thou knowest not.*

Jeremiah 33:3

*And all thy children shall be taught of the Lord;
and great shall be the peace of thy children.
In righteousness shalt thou be established: thou
shalt be far from oppression; for thou shalt not
fear: and from terror;
for it shall not come near thee.
Behold, they shall surely gather together, but not
by me: whosoever shall gather together against
thee shall fall for thy sake.*

Isaiah 54:13-15

*No weapon that is formed against thee shall
prosper; and every tongue that shall rise against
thee in judgment thou shalt condemn.*

Isaiah 54:17

For I know the thoughts that I think toward you, saith the Lord, thoughts of peace, and not of evil, to give you an expected end (hope and a future).

Jeremiah 29:11

Give, and it shall be given unto you; good measure, pressed down, and shaken together, and running over, shall men give into your bosom. For with the same measure that ye mete withal it shall be measured to you again.

Luke 6:38

But my God shall supply all your need according to his riches in glory by Christ Jesus.

Philippians 4:19

And let the peace of God rule in your hearts, to the which also ye are called in one body; and be ye thankful.

Colossians 3:15

I will never leave thee, nor forsake thee.

Hebrews 13:5b

If any of you lack wisdom, let him ask of God, that giveth to all men liberally (generously), and upbraideth not (does not find fault); and it shall be given him.

James 1:5

A Blessing for Your Children

The Lord spake unto Moses, saying, "Speak unto Aaron and unto his sons saying, On this wise ye shall bless the children of Israel,

Saying unto them:

'The Lord bless thee, and Keep thee:
The Lord make his face shine upon thee, and be gracious unto thee:
The Lord lift up his countenance upon thee, and give thee peace.'"

Numbers 6:22-26

Prayer Starter:

Lord, I know that Your word is living and active (Hebrews 4:12).

With a word, You spoke the world into being, and with words, You brought about mighty miracles. Lord, I bring to You my child/children. You said, "Bring the children to me" (Luke 18:16) and now Lord I bring _____ to You. Lord, I pray for this child. Just like the fathers of old would pray a blessing over their children, I bring this/these young one/ones to You.

Lord I ask for …

Pregnancy Prayers

Personal Notes:

Pregnancy Prayers

Section Ten:

Salvation

*Behold, I was shapen in iniquity;
and in sin did my mother conceive me.
(From my mothers womb I was sinful)*

Psalm 51:5

Pregnancy Prayers

Prayers for Salvation

Hear the voice of my supplications, when I cry unto thee, when I lift up my hands toward thy holy oracle. (Hear my cry for mercy as I call to you for help, as I lift up my hands towards your most Holy Place.)

Psalm 28:2

Truly my soul waiteth upon God: from him cometh my salvation. (My soul finds rest in God; my salvation comes from him.)

Psalm 62:1

As far as the east is from the west, so far hath He removed our transgressions from us.

Psalm 103:12

I am the door: by me if any man enter in, He shall be saved, and shall go in and out, and find pasture.(I am the gate; whoever enters through me will be saved.)

John 10:9

My sheep hear my voice, and I know them, and they follow me: And I give unto them eternal life; and they shall never perish, neither shall any man pluck them out of my hand.

John 10:27,28

Whosoever shall call on the name of the Lord shall be saved.

Acts 2:21

Believe on the Lord Jesus Christ, and thou shalt be saved, and thy house.

Acts 16:31

For He hath made him to be sin for us, who knew no sin; that we might be made the righteousness of God in him.

2 Corinthians 5:21

Are they not all ministering spirits, sent forth to minister for them who shall be heirs of salvation? (Are not all angels ministering spirits sent to serve those who will inherit salvation?)

Hebrews 1:14

Let us therefore come boldly unto the throne of grace, that we may obtain mercy, and find grace to help in time of need.

Hebrews 4:16

But God, who is rich in mercy, for his great love wherewith He loved us, Even when we were dead in sins, hath quickened us together with Christ. (Because of His great love for us, God, who is rich in mercy, made us alive with Christ even when we were dead in transgressions—it is by grace you have been saved.

Ephesians 2:4-5

Therefore if any man be in Christ, He is a new creature: old things are passed away; behold, all things are become new.

2 Corinthians 5:17

This then is the message which we have heard of him, and declare unto you, that God is light, and in him is no darkness at all. If we say that we have fellowship with him, and walk in darkness, we lie, and do not the truth:

But if we walk in the light, as He is in the light, we have fellowship one with another, and the blood of Jesus Christ his Son cleanseth us from all sin.

1 John 1:5-7

If we confess our sins, He is faithful and just to forgive us our sins, and to cleanse us from all unrighteousness.

1 John 1:9

Prayer Starters:

Lord, I know that it is not Your will that anyone should perish without the knowledge and saving grace that You extend to all mankind. Lord, I pray for my baby (and children) and ask that You would help me live a life worthy of You and bear good fruit (Colossians 1:10) of a person that has a personal relationship with You. I ask that You would give me wisdom in the areas where I lack it so that I can grow and change (James 1:5) so that I can walk a worthy Christian walk. Help me to teach the child/children Your ways (Deuteronomy 6:4-9).

Lord, You know my child/children by name; You created their inmost being and watched as they took shape in my womb. Lord, I ask that You would watch over his/her life. Thank You that every plan and purpose that You have ordained for them will come to pass. That he/she would know Your voice and follow Your word. May they grow in wisdom, stature and favour with You and man (Luke 2:52).

Lord, I also ask….

Personal Notes:

Section Eleven: Week-By-Week

The Lord shall preserve thy going out and thy coming in from this time forth, and even for evermore.

Psalm 121:8

Although I am by no means an expert of development, I find it fascinating the changes both small and rapid that take place in just 40 weeks. It is hard to comprehend the growth and development that takes place inside the foetus simultaneously. Knowing what changes are taking place can also help us to pray specifically for development.

Weeks 1-2

- About a quarter of a million sperm begin to swim through the cervix and uterus into the fallopian tubes. It takes only one to penetrate the egg (ovum) that waits there. The genetic material combine and the egg start dividing.

Week 3

- The ball of cells (blastocyst) is multiplying rapidly.

- Within the amniotic sac, fluid begins to collect. The placenta cells are also forming, producing hCG, which turns your pregnancy test positive!

Week 4

- Just about one month into the pregnancy, the cells of the placenta are tunneling into the lining of the uterus.

- The embryo is made up of two layers of cells

Week 5

- At this point, the amniotic sac is increasing in fluid. This is also why there is an increase in the volume of blood flow in your body, making you need to urinate more frequently.

- The amniotic sac houses the embryo. The embryo is made up of three layers now – the top layer will develop in the brain, spinal cord, nerves and backbone.

Week 6

- Leg and arm buds, which are paddle-shaped, are now visible.

- The heart changes from being a single tube into a complex four-chambered organ. It beats at about 160 beats per minute, which is about double the rate of your own heartbeat.

- Within the mouth, the tongue and vocal cords are forming.

- There are small depressions being formed which will later become the ear.

Week 7

- More loo stops as your blood volume increases!

- The baby is about 1 cm.

- This week eyelids cover your baby's eyes.

Week 8

- Baby is growing daily and is now about 2 cm long. At this point the baby is called a foetus.

- The lungs and breathing tube develop this week. Within the brain, neural pathways are forming, extending and connecting to one another.

- Although the hands are still webbed, the fingers are growing longer.

- The baby's legs are growing and the knee joints are being formed this week.

Week 9

- Foetus is the size of an olive. There are primitive functions of the nerves, muscles and organs.

- Fingertips are developing.

- Earlobes are visible.

- Major joints such as the shoulders, knee, ankle, wrist and elbows are able to move.

Week 10

- The baby is about 3.8 cm this week.

- The jawbone is forming with tooth buds.

- The heart is fully formed, and at this time the organs grow and mature rapidly. The baby's liver is making its own blood cells.

- The brain increases and makes the head look disproportionate to the rest of the body

- The fingers are now completely separate, too.

Week 11

- Your baby's bones start to harden, and its head makes up about one third of its total length. The baby is now approximately 4 cm long.

- All bones in the face are present and tiny tooth buds begin to form in the mouth under the gums. The tongue and palate are also present in the mouth.

- There are fingernail and toenail beds being formed. The baby can now start to move its tiny hands and can open and close its fingers.

- Hair follicles begin to form on the crown of the head.

Week 12

- The baby is about 6 cm this week. Your waist may start thickening as your uterus starts to expand. About this time, there is usually a dating scan. The skeleton is still made up of cartiledge. The baby has 300 bones as opposed to an adult's 206, because bones fuse and grow together.

- The kidneys excrete urine.

- The eyes and ears have moved more into their final positions within the head.

- The urge to urinate should be less frequent now, and the queeziness should start getting better as the weeks move on. However, this varies from person to person. Although the nausea might be subsiding, there might be an onset of dizziness while there is an increase of blood flow to your baby. As blood vessels relax and widen, the blood flow is increased to the baby. This means lower blood pressure for you and reduced blood flow to your brain.

- This dizziness could also be from low blood sugar levels if you are not eating regularly or if your cloths are too tight.

Week 13

- The foetus is about 7.7 cm. It is kicking, swallowing, yawning and hiccuping. The placenta may weigh up to an ounce now but will be about one or two pounds at birth!

- The baby's head is starting to look more in proportion with the body now, and tiny bones in the arms and legs begin to form.

- The baby starts to urinate out the amniotic fluid it has been swallowing. The organs such as the stomach and bowel grow and the vocal chords, too.

- The baby's intestines start to move into the abdominal cavity because up to now they have been housed inside a cavity in the umbilical cord.

- The baby's fingerprints are now unique.

Week 14

- By week 14 the nausea should be subsiding and you should be feeling more yourself.

- Your tummy is being pushed out by your uterus at this time. The baby is about 8cm long and is the size of your fist, weighing about 42 grams. You might be experiencing the joys of pregnancy such as nose bleeds, congestion, snoring and pregnancy brain fog which makes it difficult to remember where you last placed your keys!

- On the baby, small hairs develop, called lanugo. This hair helps to protect the baby while living in the fluid.

- Muscles and brain impulses allow the face to "practice" grimacing and frowning.

- The neck is lengthening and the arms are more in proportion with the body this week, although the legs still have some growing to do.

Week 15

- This week your baby has grown to the size of an orange.

- Air sacs in the lungs are encouraged in their development as the baby inhales and exhales the amniotic fluid.

- The baby can start to sense light through the eyelids this week. The developing taste buds can "taste" what you eat.

- Joints and limbs can move. The legs start looking longer than the arms as they start to grow in proportion.

Week 16

- Four months into the pregnancy!

- Tiny bones in the ears make it likely that the baby could start hearing your voice from about this point

- The head starts to look more upright as the back muscles become stronger and the body grows more and more in proportion. The nervous system is branching out through out the body.

- Baby is roughly 10 cm long. There is a lot of flexing and stretching of the baby's limbs. On ultrasound, the baby may be seen to suck its thumb.

- The heart is beating and pumping blood around the body.

- Toenails develop

Week 17

- The baby could weigh about 150 grams now and be about 11.5 cm in length.

- The soft cartilage is changing to bone. Body fat is starting to be deposited and this will continue till the end of your pregnancy.

- The face is looking proportionate, and as the eyebrows and eyelashes develop, their face takes on a human appearance.

- Although their eyes are still fused shut, the eyeballs can move in the sockets. Their sense of hearing is developing, too, which could make them start at the sound of loud noises

- The baby's heartbeat is regulated by the brain and can be beating between 140-160 beats per minute.

- Sweat glands are beginning to develop.

- The umbilical cord continues to grow and strengthen though the weeks.

- As your stomach grows, your center of gravity changes, making you feel off balance.

Week 18

- There might be the faint fluttering of movements, which can be felt by you from about this time.

- At about size of a bell pepper, roughly 14 cm long and about 200 grams, your baby is growing and becoming more active. They can kick and move about, as well as suck their thumbs and hold onto the umbilical cord.

- Myelin, a protective covering around the nerves starts to form. This covering helps the nerves send messages to one another.

- At this time, little baby girls will already be forming eggs in her ovaries.

Week 19

- Baby could weigh about half a pound in weight, although some babies will be heavier and some will be less so.

- Neurons are connected between the brain and muscles.

- Cartlidge is beginning to harden into bone.

- Towards the second half of pregnancy, vernix starts to form on the skin. This is formed from the dead skin cells and oils secreted from the skin. The lanugo (fine hair covering) holds the vernix in place. Vernix is thought to be a natural skin cleanser, anti-infective, antioxidant, moisturiser and wound healer! The vernix helps protect the baby's sensitive skin while sitting in the amniotic fluid and starts to shed as the birth date draws near. However, some babies are born with remnants on their skin, which can be washed off at the first bath.

Week 20

- HALF WAY THERE!!!!

- Well done! At this point in the pregnancy, your baby could measure about 25 cm long and weight as much as 10 ounces, he/she is starting to grow now. Baby is still practicing swallowing and now is also producing myconium which will make up his/her first nappy. There is still plenty of room for baby to move about

- The baby's nerves in the brain are still developing. These will control the sense of smell, seeing, hearing, touching and tasting.

- As your bump begins to grow, the ligaments on the sides of your stomach begin to stretch, which may cause some aches or pains. Pain might also develop in the pelvis. Sleeping comfortably might also start to become an issue, too. Heartburn, indigestion and leg cramps may be common problems, too.

Week 21

- Each day, baby swallows some amniotic fluids. This helps provide nutrition and hydration and helps the baby to practice digestion and swallowing. In doing this, the baby also gets a range of the tastes of foods that you eat.

- Although there are lots of movements happening, Baby is sleeping about 12-14 hours a day.

- Varicose veins may be prevented or reduced by putting your legs up when you sit and sleep on your left side. You can also wear support hosiery for pregnancy.

Week 22

- Still growing, but at this time baby could be about 27 cm long and about the size of a papaya.

- The organs continue to grow. The pancreas is producing essential hormones and their lungs are developing, too. Baby might have sprouted some white locks on its head, due to the lack of pigmentation.

- Baby might have their daily routine of sleep and wake and can also perceive light and dark much better now. too.

- Lips, eyelids, and eyebrows are becoming more distinct. Baby can hear the sound of your heart, your blood moving around your body, and the sound of your voice.

- Wear comfortable shoes and put your legs up when possible.

Week 23

- Your baby could weigh about 500 grams now and be about 30 cm long. The bulking out will take place in the next few weeks.

- Loud noises could startle baby at this point but more familiar voices will be more soothing.

- As your belly grows, beware of back ache, clumsiness and put your feet up when you can.

- Baby's heartbeat can be heard through a handheld monitor.

Week 24

- The baby could weigh about 600 grams this week.

- The lungs are mature enough to breath in air if needed. Branches of the respiratory and cells that produce surfactant will help air sacs inflate once air is breathed.

- The sense of hearing continues to develop.

Week 25

- This week, the baby's skin is less translucent and looking a bit more pinker. This is because capillaries are forming under the skin and filling with blood. Around this time, blood vessels also develop in the lungs.

- Baby's nostrils, which have been closed up till now, will start to open this week. This allows the foetus to take practice breaths.

- Baby continues to grow, and at this point in pregnancy, it may be an idea to think about the type of birth you want.

- Drink plenty of water and rest when you feel tired.

Week 26

- By now, your baby could weigh as much as 2 pounds and can be as long as 35.5 cm long.

- This week the eyes are beginning to open. Up to now, they have remained shut as the retina has been developing. The iris at this stage still doesn't have much colour.

- Nerves to the ear have had time to develop further, and it could be possible that baby can hear both yours and those around you. The baby can also respond to noise it can hear.

- The baby continues to lay down fat deposits. Over the coming weeks, the space in the stomach will become more cramped. There might even be more of a pattern of times of the day when the baby is more and less active.

Week 27

- Third And Final Trimester!

- Baby could weigh about 850-900 grams and be about 36 cm long. Baby likes to have a wriggle but feels secure in a slightly curled position.

- Although the ears are still covered in vernix, the baby can hear the voices and sounds in its environment.

- At this time, the baby has very developed and more taste buds now than when it come into the whole. You may feel hiccuping!

Week 28

- The baby can be about 16 inches (36 cm) and about 2.5 pounds (1 kg). Not only are the eyes open but the baby practices blinking.

- Baby continues to practice breathing, sucking, hiccuping. All are important for development and for skills in the outside world.

- Baby not only develops its own sleep/wake cycle but may also be dreaming.

- Fat layers continue to form. The bones are nearly developed but still soft and pliable. These will harden after the birth.

Week 29

- Your baby will weigh roughly three pounds at this time and in the next few weeks will almost double its weight.

- Lung muscles continue to mature and the head is also growing bigger to make room for the developing brain.

- The buds for permanent teeth are forming in the gums.

- You will also need plenty of calcium, vitamin C, protein and iron as his bones are soaking up calcium.

Week 30

- As your baby grows, so does your pregnant belly. Baby will be gaining about half a pound each week from now on.

- Up until now, the brain was smooth but now the surface is taking on the grooves and indentations. These wrinkles allow for increased amount of brain tissue.

- The brain and increased amount of fat mean that the lanugo starts to disappear.

- The bone marrow also begins to take over production of the red blood cells.

- The digestive tract is now almost fully developed.

Week 31

- At just over 3 pounds and about 24 inches (40 cm) long, the baby will continue to gain weight. The arms, legs and body fill out as the fat layers accumulate. This makes them look more in proportion to the head

- He/she can turn its head from side to side.

- The brain is developing very fast as connections between the nerve cells are being formed. The baby is using all this development to process information, tract light, and receive information from its five senses.

Week 32

- Baby could weigh almost 3 1/2 - 4 pounds now. Fat continues to accumulate. The skin becomes more opaque and less wrinkled.

- The digestive system is all ready to go, and there has been much practicing with sucking, moving and swallowing.

- There are now toenails, fingernails and "hair".

- The space is starting to become more cramped inside the womb and usually by this point, the head is down.

Week 33

- Baby could measure anywhere from 17-19 inches, growing atleast another inch this week. The buffereing system is diminishing as baby grows. At this point, there is probably more baby than amniotic fluid, and those pokes and kicks are being felt in a big way.

- The head bones won't fuse together, making it easier to come through the birthcanal. These bones won't fuse till early adulthood, because the brain and tissues grow through childhood. The rest of the bones in the body are hardening.

- The immune system is fully developed.

Week 34

- Baby could be weighing about 5 pounds now.

- The central nervous system continues to mature and the lungs are maturing.

- In most cases, a male's testicles are making their way down from his abdomen to his scrotum.

- Baby's sense of hearing is well developed now and probably enjoys hearing your voice.

Week 35

- 20 inches and about 5 ½ pounds this week as your delivery date approaches. In the middle of pregnancy, a baby's fat percentage is about 2%. Now it is closer to 15% and by due date will be roughly 30%.

- Thoughts of labour are probably more at the forefront of your mind than anything.

Week 36

- Growth rate begins to slow down at this time.

- Most of the baby's systems are mature–blood circulation, immune system. However, the digestive system is not fully mature till some time after birth.

Week 37

- If your baby was born now, it would still be considered early term. The next couple weeks are allowing the lungs and brain to mature fully.

- Baby could be a bout 6-7 pounds in weight, still rolling and wiggling about.

- At this time, the baby's head will at birth be the same circumference as their hips, abdomen and shoulders.

- You could be experiencing Braxton hicks.

Week 38

- Your baby could be weighing 7 pounds or more at this stage. If born now, it will be considered at term.

- Vernix and lanugo continue to shed from the body.

- The baby swallows the amniotic fluid along with dead cells and this is what will make up the merconium (first bowel movement).

- The lungs continue to mature and secrete surfactant, which prevents the air sacs in the lungs from sticking to one another once breathing starts.

- More fat continues to accumulate, and fine tuning in the brain continues to occur.

Week 39

- It's all a waiting game if baby hasn't arrived by now. The size won't change much in these last couple weeks. By now, frustration may have set in or you're just enjoying the rest that you can enjoy before the joyous arrival of your little one.

Section Twelve: Our Story

My Heart in His Hands

When my father and my mother forsake me, then the Lord will take me up.

(Even if your father and mother forsake you, The Lord is always there).

Psalm 27:10

Pregnancy Prayers

How It All Started

"There is something wrong with the heart," were the last things I heard the specialist say as I watched the black and white screen with my 22 week old baby girl wriggling and squirming.

To me, that was the precious life of my fourth child, not just a bunch of cells that had gone wrong. The sonographer then had to call a consultant, and we were ushered into another waiting room. The consultant had a look. There was no chat as she was having a really good look. We were told to wait outside and someone would come to see us. We were taken into another room where the lady had a more advanced scan machine as she wanted to check blood flow, etc. She said that there looked to be a heart complication. The heart had not been formed properly, and there only seemed to be *one vein from the heart to lungs.*

Without more detail, the expert could reveal no more to us, but we were informed that we could expect to be contacted by a hospital in London who would be able to take our case.

A few days later, we got the call. We had an appointment at a Children's Hospital in London. As there was a specialist unit, we would be able to get the full picture of what was wrong and then take it from there. I remember us praying in faith on the way to the hospital that actually all would be well and that the defect would be minor and that the operation would require little or no operation.

How wrong we were!

One's gut instinct that things really aren't well is when the scan takes double the time and the consultant can't look you in the eye and the words, "Let's go to the consultation room" take on a whole new meaning.

As my husband and I sat there, it was almost like the consultant rolled out a scroll as the defect list went on and on. My husband sat in shock. I just cried. Besides the heart not being formed properly, they could not detect veins from heart to lungs. I realized at this moment that I should have paid more attention in school during the study about the heart anatomy. It all sounded like a bad dream. To top it all off, with this condition there are further complications within the body, organs on the wrong side, multiple spleens and a malrotated bowel.

The last thought as we were left sitting in a box room left to think and wait for some sweet tea were the words "There are other options" and "You will have the chance to say goodbye."

"Oh, my God, why are you doing this to us?" was a thought going around in my mind. I thought God was good; I thought we would come away today with positive news.... What did I do wrong to deserve this? After the shock wore off, we walked to the car not really knowing what to say or do. However, I do remember us looking at each other and saying, "We will have a miracle." We would endeavor to trust God. We did not accept this news. and the next scan in a couple weeks would reveal more.

I could barely look at the paperwork the next morning and opened the booklet advice on termination, then shut it, berating myself for even holding it in my hands but realized, too, that after the news we had heard a few hours before, many people would have chosen this option, knowing that the road ahead would not be easy. The pain, the upset. I sobbed for those babies not born and for the people who were in the same situation.

Why God?

"For my thoughts are not your thoughts, nor your ways my ways "(Isaiah 55:8).

There would be no one to hold our hands and no one to say it would be okay. It was us and our three children standing in what seemed an open desert with no paths or direction but us just walking together. Not by sight, just a pure faith walk that God would come through for us.

It is in this time when you have no fallback, when there is no backup plan of your own worldly advances that the question of how much faith you have comes into play. As a family, we determined to trust God and we would believe for a miracle.

I'm not a prayer warrior nor an intercessor. I am but a mother desperate to see God's hand at work and for Him to be gracious and save my daughter's life. Lamentations 2:19 says, "Lift up your hands to the Lord for the lives of your children… like water for the lives of your young children." This we did. In Lamentations it says during the night watches we can call out to the Lord. My husband and I would put on healing music and watch broadcasts of healings and we would pray and stir our faith. This was our battle and no one was going to do the praying for us.

After the initial scan at the London hospital, we had to go back about two weeks later because as the foetus grew, they could take detailed video of the heart and maybe start thinking of what they could do for surgery as they suspected she would have to go onto life support after delivery. This was a rare case, and the specialists wanted to be prepared. I remember the lady saying to us after one of the scans that what was amazing was that despite all these complications, the heartbeat strong and steady.

We continued to pray. I poured out my heart during the night watches. I remember being up at midnight, 3 a.m., 5 a.m. and just praying, sometimes begging God.

Before each scan, we said, "Today we will see the miracle,. Today we will come out after seeing shocked doctors' faces saying, 'There is nothing wrong. We made a mistake.'" However, the miracle did not happen how we had hoped or planned. BUT at 25 weeks, we had another scan and the consultant thought she saw ONE, NEW vein to the heart!

We were thrilled! That made two veins to the heart. We committed ourselves to a ten day fruit and vegetable fast, determined to seek The Lord.

Soon after this, we had to go to a local hospital where one of the consultants worked as a locum a few days a week. He was going to do a scan on the bowels and see if there were multiple spleens. The scan was lengthy but it appeared that there was only one spleen and the bowel appeared normal. There were no extra or mirrored organs as they suspected.

Between 30-32 weeks, we went for a private scan, a detailed 3-D scan and explained to the consultant what was wrong. This scan revealed a THIRD vein from heart to lungs. We rejoiced afterward and felt very positive.

Pregnancy Prayers

As the due date approached, preparations were made with baby clothes and birthing plans, what we would expect to happen, and what to prepare ourselves for.

At 39 weeks and a couple days, I sat in the hospital for two days because I had to be induced, and they were waiting for a bed to be free in the children's ICU. At last, the time arrived and within two hours of induction, I was allowed a brief cuddle with my new daughter and then Dad rushed off with the doctors to the ICU. I showered and dressed and then went to see her while she was having scans done. For the next couple hours, I could only give her hand a squeeze and then even to hold her brought complications with wires, etc. As she was breathing on her own, we were able to leave within three days with an appointment the following week to check the bowels.

That appointment was another success! The bowels were normal and no operation would be needed.

At two months, our daughter had an initial operation and they felt that they needed to wait a bit longer to hopefully let her get stronger. At this time, she was still wearing newborn clothing and had to be fed with special baby milk. We were so thrilled that she was taking some food – even if it was just 100 ml a day. Some days I fed her with a syringe, just to get down 100 ml of the milk.

At this time we moved houses, too.

A few months down the line, she got a really bad cold. Initially, we took her to our local doctor who said everything was fine and that she just needed some antibiotics. After two days ,she just slept, didn't eat and couldn't even lift her head.

My husband took her to the hospital. It was serious. If we had waited any longer.... I raced up to the hospital, and my husband and I ran up to the child care unit. I just remember seeing wires and people. I couldn't even see my little girl on the bed for all the activity. The hospital in London was contacted and they prepared a bed for her. I remember her being wheeled out in almost a chamber with heart monitors and sitting in the ambulance just praying. We were in the hospital for nearly two weeks, my husband and I took turns to stay with by her bedside. However, at the end, my son and I became ill with a virus and had to go home. My husband slept at her bedside.

Amazingly, she came home on Christmas Eve, and we could celebrate together.

During this time, we had little help or support from family, but God was so faithful. He put us in touch with a lady who introduced us to a few members of a small church near the area we had just moved to. They came and met with us at our home and prayed with us. We knew the big operation was coming and coming soon. The doctors said they couldn't wait any longer. A date was set and we moved into a Ronald McDonald house in London.

Amazingly, our elderly neighbors said they would look after our dog while we were away, so that was one less thing to worry about.

We did a mini-fast at the start of the new year and a 21 day fast which finished the evening of the operation day, which we feel is what helped us with the peace and direction we needed these last three weeks. We were also grateful to drink some coffee which kept us awake for all those days and nights.

On Monday March 12th, we arrived in London for the pre-op assessment, scans and blood tests and meeting with the surgeon.

Early on Tuesday the 13th of March, we prayed, said goodbye, and my husband took her to be washed and dressed for the six hour operation which would follow. The surgery was new, unique to her case, and we just waited with our children playing in the waiting room. We drank coffee, watched the clock and prayed.

We got the call that she was in recovery and clean up. We had to wait almost an hour and as we walked into the NICU. I can still remember the smells. We had seen her with tubes and cuts before, but this was hectic and I remember just standing there crying. In my mind I wondered why God was letting this happen. The surgeon came to see us and said that there was still a small leak in one of the valves but that this should not affect anything.

She seemed to do well, and after two days they decided that she could come off the life support.

We were thrilled. Things were progressing well and our prayers were being answered. Before the operation, the cardiologist said she would be on the life support for at least 4 days to give the heart and body a time to adjust to being fixed, and here after two days we were looking ahead to recovery on the unit and home!

Not long after she was left to breathe on her own, it all seemed to go downhill. Her chest was heaving and we could see her heart racing in her chest. Her chest and stomach got bigger and she got greyer and greyer in colour. She was put back on life support. X-rays showed her heart to be dramatically enlarged. In fact, even though she was on a large dose of morphine, she had not slept for two days as she fought for breath. The enlarged heart was laying on the lungs and compressing it. Not only this, but the broncci of the lungs were also compressed. They were worried. They contacted the on-call cardiologist and scanning and tests began. We continued to pray throughout her operation and stayed in the hospital. We had healing scriptures under her pillow which were replaced with every bedding change. When we were able, we put our phones on beside her with healing scriptures being played into her ears.

She was put back on life support, and by the morning she was moved right next to the doctors' station. On Monday afternoon, she had a cardioscope, a delicate procedure which is done under anesthetic. Basically, it is one spaghetti-like catheter inserted into either side of the groin, and it goes up a leg vein to the heart where it measures heart pressures. After 2 hours they came back with no answer.

They were baffled.

The next scan was an MRI down through the throat to get 3D images of the heart. They thought the valve that was initially leaking after the first op was a cause but still they could not pin-point the cause. At this point our little girl was losing more weight and every few hours she had more tests for minerals and what the body was low on. She began to look like a pin cushion. At one point they wanted to shave her head and put a drip into a vein in the head. My sons were sitting next to me on the floor. It was a Saturday evening and there was noting to do but pray and ask they find another vein. Gratefully, they made multiple attempts and secured a vein which had not previously been used.

On Tuesday morning while she was still on life support, the doctor came to us and said they had absolutely no clue what was going on. With the heart fixed, they could not understand why she could not breathe. At this point, my husband came to take over as I called Meg, one of the ladies from the church and she said the church would start praying. My husband came and I couldn't even speak as the consultant relayed what he had initially told me. At the moment, I had to escape to the chapel within the hospital. I had to be alone and pray, cry out – could God not hear my silent prayers? There were two doors but they were both locked. It was like looking at a place of sanctuary and not being able to get in. It was how I felt, just waiting. I sat on the bench with my head in my hands, "Oh, God, please just help!"

There was a voice next to me, a security guard. He asked what I was looking for and I said I just wanted to pray. He didn't have the key but he could get it for me….. no, I just needed some time, at this point, he turned to mbe and said "all will be well."

I do believe it was an angel.

We had some days of waiting. The nurses did what they had to but no one knew what to say to us. We prayed for an answer, that God would reveal to us what the problem was. That day we got a message from Meg that the pastor from their church "just happened" to be in London for a course and he felt the Lord said he should come and anoint Michaela like in James 5.

Well, this sparked off a series of God events! That night he came and we prayed over her. We all stood around her bed and prayed and Neil anointed her. I then took the boys back to the hostel where we slept. We prayed and they went to sleep.

When all was quiet in the room, I just prayed. As I prayed, the Lord reminded me of a dream I had a couple weeks before we came to the hospital. It was me in a swampy area, and as I looked across the swamp, I saw my daughter in a swamp with a black python wrapping itself around her neck and squeezing the breath out of her. I realized that this was what was happening to her now. She could not breathe! I proceded to prayed and sent a message to my husband to tell him what was happening and he should pray over her and bind the spirit of death and suffocation.

He prayed and he said afterwards the alarm on the life support machine went off indicating a change of breathing rate. She was breathing deeper! The nurse on that night was a Christian, too. She had just come onto shift after Neil had been there, and she allowed him to stand and pray with our daughter.

The breathing got steadier as the night progressed. We shared our news with Meg and Ceri. As Wednesday came, we now began to ask the Lord for clarity and to clearly show us the problem. He knew, but the doctors didn't!

Pregnancy Prayers

Thursday morning at 8:15 a.m., a specialist in the hospital heard about Michaela's case and said he "happened to have 15minutes to spare" and would come look at Michaela. He usually did heart scans on babies. I was standing at the bedside and the scanning monitor was brought round. It was literally within minutes that he saw the problem—the aorta or a large vein still had two holes in it. After a few beats of the heart, the two holes would open together and let blood into the lungs.

He called the surgeon, and it was suddenly like everyone and everything came alive around us. The surgeon, who had done the initial surgery came to see us, saying he wanted to operate as soon as possible. Twenty minutes later, he came to us saying that another baby had just gone sick and an operating theatre had become available. After the initial fussing and preparations for the next lot of surgery, we sat three hours later just waiting.

On Sunday 25th after the operation, an X-ray showed a cloud on the upper left lung. The doctors were not sure what it was, but we prayed and on Monday morning the cloud had dispersed and her lungs were clear.

On Monday 26th she was taken off life support and breathing well on her own. We had a consultation with the surgeon. The consultant whose care she was under in the hospital said that if it had not been for the leak in the valve after the initial operation that she would have probably not made it, as the leak helped release some of the pressure in the heart!

I remember the day a few days after being on the ward, we were allowed to have a single room so that her brothers could have some where to sit with us and we were offered lunch off the food trolley. I had some mash, peas and fishfingers. I was sitting next to her as she was being propped up by some pillows. She was bright-faced and had pink cheeks. She reached over to get some mash! I put the plate in front of her and she started taking little fist fulls of mash potato. I grabbed my phone to take some pictures of my child eating. At this precise moment the doctor walked in and asked why did we all look so shocked. I said it was the first time we had actually seen her hungry and eating!

She was initially put onto medication and had a heart type monitor when we returned home. We prayed about this, too. After the initial consultation post-op, she was taken off all medication and did not have to have a monitor.

She was on medication to support a good rhythm for the heart, but after the first consultation, the doctor said they would trial it without the medication. She no longer has medication, just check ups with the consultants. It has taken some time to write this story and re-live that year. We went through heartache and weeks of sleepless nights but we know without doubt that God is faithful. We realize that Bible-type miracles still happen today

This is not just our testimony but hers, too. Who is like the Lord! The Lord did a miracle right before our eyes. His name be praised. (Psalm 146)

I think the following Psalm is one of the most beautiful Psalms. When I read the first line, I can almost just stop with a sigh of praise afterward because He is our hope and the lover of our souls in times of troubles and distress. The mighty, powerful God himself comes down from the Heavens to rescue us and keep our feet from slipping. With His aid we are strengthened to fight the enemy. We can see that our bodies are strengthened with his great everlasting power.

During this time, this Psalm was constantly before my eyes. He aids us against our enemies. He is in the boat during our storms.

I am ever grateful for His mercies which are new daily or I could not stand. I am ever dependent that He keeps no record of my sin—or who could stand. Alas, I cannot say, like David, did in this Psalm that it is because of my righteousness or clean hands that He has saved my daughter but because of His unfailing love for us.

Thank You, Lord.

I love you, Lord, my strength.

*The lord is my rock, in who I take refuge,
My shield and the horn of my salvation,
my stronghold.
I call to the lord, who is worthy of praise,
And I have been saved from my enemies.
The cords of death entangled me;
The torrents of destruction overwhelmed me.
The cords of the grave coiled around me;
And the snares of death confronted me.
In my distress I called to the lord;
I cried to my God for help.
From his temple He heard my voice;
My cry came before him, into his ears.
The earth trembled and quaked,
And the foundations of the mountains shook;
They trembled because He was angry.
Smoke rose from his nostrils;
Consuming fire came from his mouth,
Burning coals blazed out of it.
He parted the heavens and came down;
Dark clouds were under his feet.
He mounted the cherubim and flew;
He soared on the wings of the wind.
He made darkness his covering,
his canopy around him-
The dark rain clouds of the sky.
Out of the brightness of
his presence clouds advanced,
With hailstones and bolts of lightening.
The lord thundered from heaven;*

The voice of the most high resounded.
He shot his arrows and scattered the enemy,
With great bolts of lightning.
The lord thundered from heaven;
The voice of the most high resounded.
He shot his arrows and scattered the enemy,
With great bolts of lightening He routed them.
The valleys of the sea were exposed
And the foundations of the earth laid bare
At your rebuke, Lord,
At the blast of breath from your nostrils.
He reached down from on high
and took hold of me;
He drew me out of deep waters.
He rescued me from my powerful enemy,
From my foes, who were too strong for me.
They confronted me in the day of disaster,
But the lord was my support.
He brought me out into a spacious place;
He rescued me because He delighted in me.
The lord dealt with me according
to my righteousness;
According to the cleanness
of my hands He rewarded me
For I have kept the ways of the lord;
I am not guilty of turning from my God.
All his laws are before me;
I have not turned away from his decrees.
I have been blameless before him
And I have kept myself from sin.

The lord has rewarded me
according to my righteousness
According to the cleanness of
my hands in his sight.
To the faithful you show your self faithful,
To the blameless you show yourself blameless,
To the pure you show yourself pure,
But to the devious you show yourself shrewd.
You save the humble
But bring low those whose eyes are haughty.
You, lord, keep my lamp burning;
My God turns my darkness into light.
With your help I can advance against a troop;
With my God I can scale a wall.
As for God, his way is perfect:
The Lord's word is flawless;
He shields all who take refuge in him.
For who is God besides the lord?
And who is the Rock except our God?
It is God who arms me with strength
And keeps my way secure.
He makes my feet like the feet of a deer;
He causes me to stand on the heights.
He trains my hands for battle;
My arms can bend a bow of bronze.
You make your saving help my shield,
And your right hand sustains me;
Your help has made me great.
You provide a broad a broad path for my feet,
So that my ankles do not give way.

*I pursued my enemies and overtook them;
I did not turn back till they were destroyed.
I crushed them so that they could not rise;
They fell beneath my feet.
You armed me with strength for battle;
You humbled my adversaries before me.
You made my enemies turn their backs in flight,
And I destroyed my foes.*

Psalm 18: 1-40 (NIV)

*Contend, Lord, with those who contend with
me; fight against those who fight against me.
Take up shield and armor;
arise and come to my aid.
Brandish spear and javelin against those who
pursue me. Say to me, "I am your salvation."
May those who seek my life be disgraced and
put to shame; may those who plot my ruin
be turned back in dismay.
May they be like chaff before the wind, with the
angel of the Lord driving them away;
may their path be dark and slippery, with the
angel of the Lord pursuing them.
Since they hid their net for me without cause
and without cause dug a pit for me,
may ruin overtake them by surprise—may the
net they hid entangle them,
may they fall into the pit, to their ruin.
Then my soul will rejoice in the Lord*

and delight in his salvation.
My whole being will exclaim,
"Who is like you, Lord?
You rescue the poor from those
too strong for them, the poor and needy
from those who rob them."

Psalm 35:1-10 (NIV)

I call to the lord, who is worthy of praise, And I am saved from my enemies.

Psalm 18:3 (NIV)

Pregnancy Prayers

References

What To Expect

www.WhatToExpect.com

Bounty

www.Bounty.com

www.ingramcontent.com/pod-product-compliance
Lightning Source LLC
LaVergne TN
LVHW011837060526
838200LV00053B/4072